Super Safari 2

Letters and Numbers Workbook

Colour in Leo!

CAMBRIDGE
UNIVERSITY PRESS

Shaftesbury Road, Cambridge CB2 8EA, United Kingdom

One Liberty Plaza, 20th Floor, New York, NY 10006, USA

477 Williamstown Road, Port Melbourne, VIC 3207, Australia

314–321, 3rd Floor, Plot 3, Splendor Forum, Jasola District Centre, New Delhi – 110025, India

103 Penang Road, #05-06/07, Visioncrest Commercial, Singapore 238467

Cambridge University Press & Assessment is a department of the University of Cambridge.

We share the University's mission to contribute to society through the pursuit of education, learning and research at the highest international levels of excellence.

www.cambridge.org
Information on this title: www.cambridge.org/9781316628171

First published 2016

20 19 18 17 16 15 14

Printed in Great Britain by CPI Group (UK) Ltd, Croydon CR0 4YY

A catalogue record for this publication is available from the British Library

ISBN 978-1-316-62817-1 Paperback

Additional resources for this publication at www.cambridge.org/supersafari

Super Safari 2
Letters and Numbers
Workbook

Hello!

The children draw themselves inside the frame. Write each child's name on the line with a yellow marker. The children trace the letters, first with their index fingers and then with different coloured crayons several times.

1 Draw and trace.

I'm _____ .

1 Count and trace.

The children point to the numbers and name them. Then they count the objects aloud. Finally, the children trace over the dotted lines from the numbers to the objects.

1

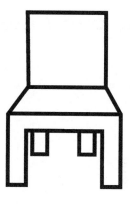

2

3

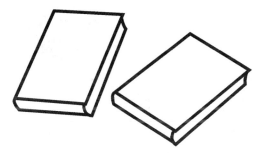

1 My school

Present the letter. The children trace and write the letters with different coloured crayons. Finally, the children colour the apple freely.

1 Trace and write. Colour the picture.

1 Count and trace. Colour the objects.

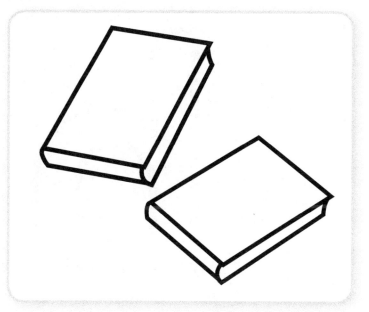

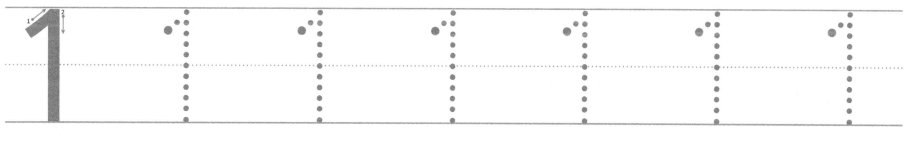

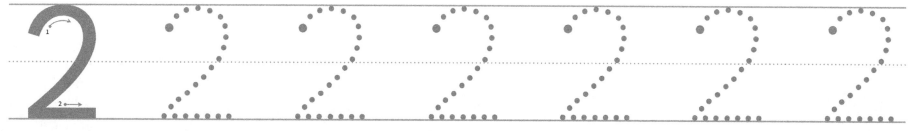

1 **Trace and write. Finger-paint.**

Present the letter. Then the children trace and write the letters with different coloured crayons. Finally, the children finger-paint the bananas.

b

1 Count and trace. Colour the objects.

3 - - - - - - - - - - - -

4 - - - - - - - - - - - -

3

4

1 Trace and write. Colour the pictures.

Present the letter. Then the children trace and write the letters with different coloured crayons. Finally, the children colour the cow and letter freely.

C   C   C   C   C   C   C

C

1 **Count and colour. Trace the numbers.**

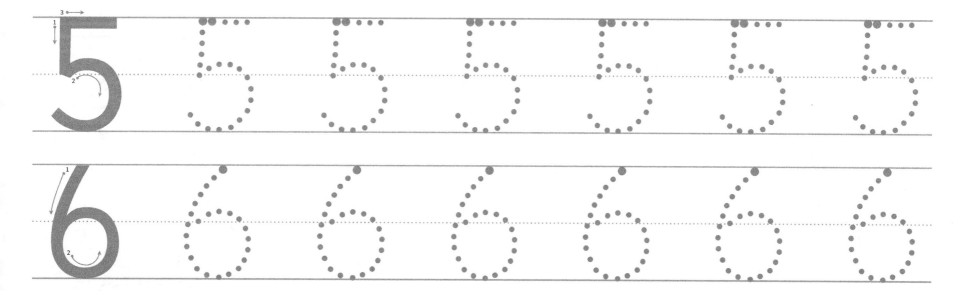

1 **Trace and colour.**

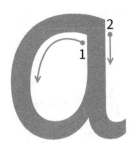

c<u>a</u>t

d<u>a</u>d

1 Colour the objects. Cut and glue.

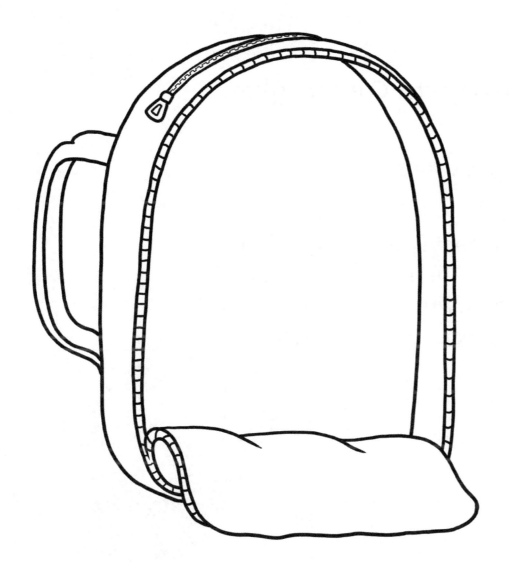

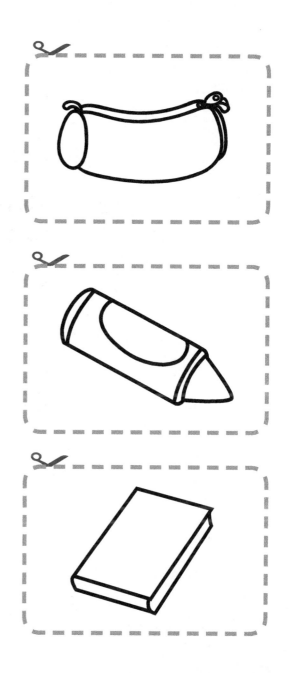

Colour the objects. Cut and glue.

Materials:

scissors, glue, crayons

Instructions:

The children identify the bag and the school objects. Then they colour and cut out the objects. Finally, the children glue the school objects inside the bag.

1 **Look and colour.**

The children point to the desk on the left side of the page. Then they find the other desk in the row. The children colour the desk. Continue in the same manner with the pencil case and the sheet of paper.

   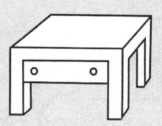 

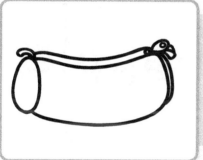    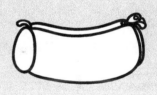

Present the letter. The children colour the pictures for the words that start with the letter "d". The children trace and write the letters with different coloured crayons.

1 Colour the pictures. Trace and write.

dinosaur

dog

apple

1 **Count and colour. Trace the numbers.**

Present the numbers. The children count the circles in each number and colour them. Then the children trace the numbers with different coloured crayons.

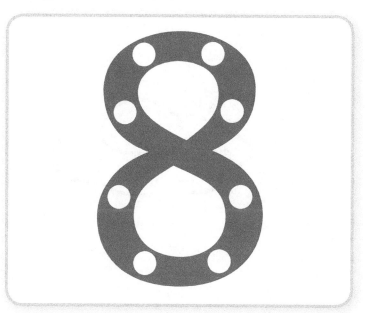

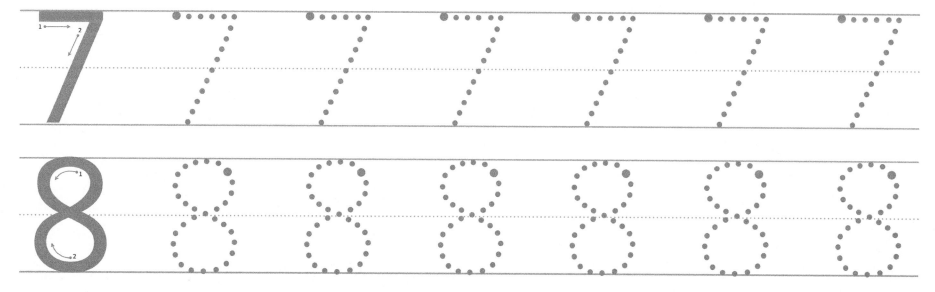

1 **Colour the letters. Trace and write.**

Present the letter. The children look at the letters in the box and colour the letters "e". Then the children trace and write the letters with different coloured crayons.

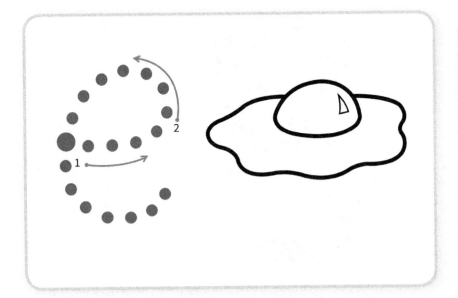

1 **Draw, trace and write.**

Present the number. Then the children draw the corresponding number of balls inside each box. The children trace and write the numbers with different coloured crayons.

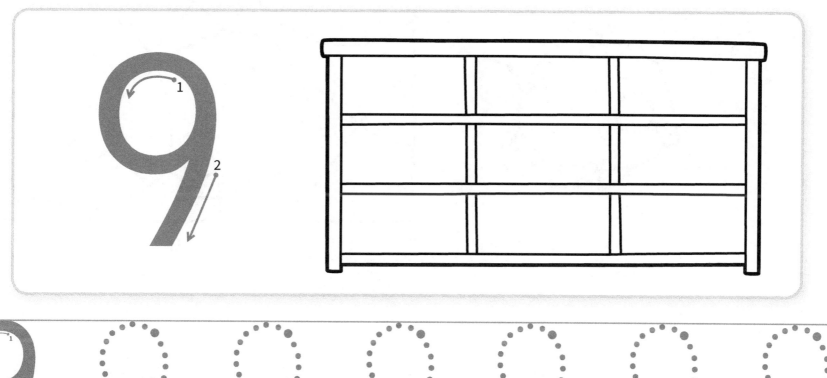

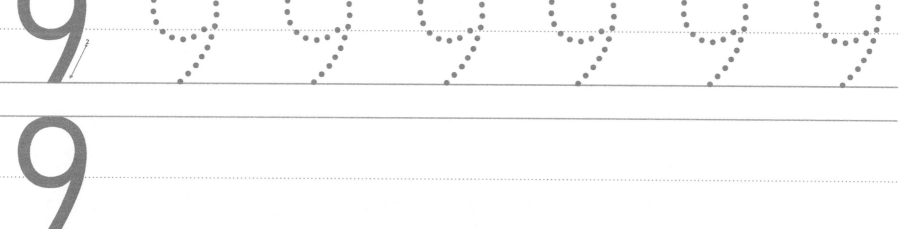

1 **Find and colour the fish. Trace and write.**

1 ## Count and colour the fingers. Trace.

Present the number. Then the children count and colour the fingers. Finally, the children trace and write the numbers with different coloured crayons.

10

10 10 10 10 10 10 10

10

1 **Match and colour.**

Ask the children to point to the first picture and say /ɪ/ – /ɪ/ – /ɪ/ – pin. Repeat the procedure with lip and sit. The children match the pictures to the words. Finally, they colour the pictures.

s**i**t

p**i**n

l**i**p

1 Colour, cut and assemble.

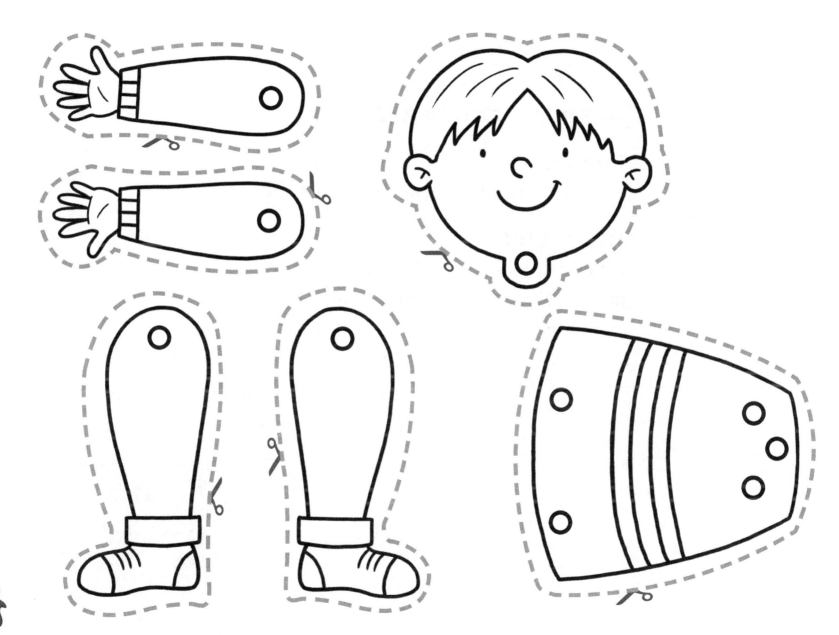

Colour, cut and assemble.

Materials:
scissors, crayons, paper fastener clips

Instructions:
The children look at the body parts, identify them and colour them. Then they cut them out and assemble the boy's body using paper fastener clips.

1 **Match the body parts.**

The children trace a line from the left hand to the right hand with their fingers first. Continue in the same manner with the rest of the body parts. Then the children trace lines with different coloured crayons.

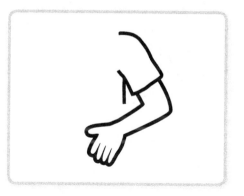

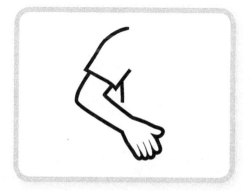

Present the letter. The children trace and write the letters with different coloured crayons. Finally, the children colour the gorilla freely.

1 **Trace and write. Colour the picture.**

g   g   g   g   g   g

g

1 **Count and colour the pictures. Trace.**

1 **Trace and write. Finger-paint.**

Present the letter. The children trace and write the letters with different coloured crayons. Next, they dip their fingers in yellow finger paint and print their fingerprints along the letter "h" and the hat.

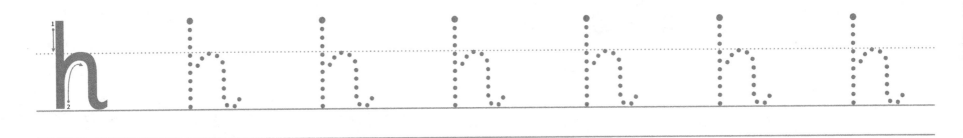

1 **Count and colour the pictures. Trace.**

Present the number. Then the children count the dolls and colour them freely. Finally, the children trace the numbers with different coloured crayons.

1 **Colour the letter and the picture. Trace and write.**

Present the letter. Next, the children colour the letter "i" and the igloo freely. Then the children trace and write the letters with different coloured crayons.

1 **Count and circle. Trace. Colour the pictures.**

The children count the dolls and circle the corresponding number. Repeat the same procedure for the puzzles. Then the children trace the numbers with different coloured crayons. Finally, the children colour the pictures freely.

11 / 12

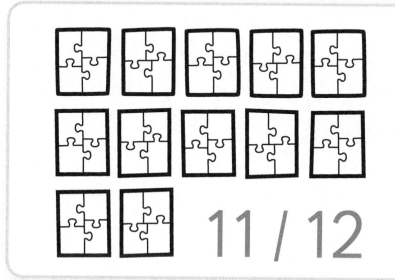

11 / 12

1 **Trace. Colour the pictures.**

e

b<u>e</u>d

e

p<u>e</u>n

1 Paint the box. Colour the toys. Cut out and assemble.

Paint the box. Colour the toys. Cut out and assemble.

Materials:
scissors, paint, brushes, crayons

Instructions:
The children paint the toy box. Then they colour the toys with coloured crayons. Next, they cut out the strip and make two slots in the toy box. Help the children insert the strip through the slots and pull on it from side to side to move the figures. Finally, the children name the toys in the toy box.

1 Listen and draw.

Say *Point to the toy box*. The children follow the instruction. Draw a ball in a toy box on the board. Ask *Where is the ball? In the toy box. Draw a ball in the toy box*. Repeat the procedure with *Draw a book under the table.*

4 In the jungle

Present the letter. Then the children colour the pictures of the words that start with the letter "j". Finally, the children trace and write the letters with different coloured crayons.

1 Colour the pictures. Trace and write.

jacket

hat

jet

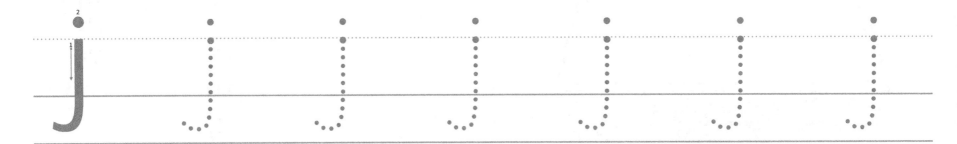

j

j

1 **Count and colour the pictures. Trace.**

Present the number. The children count the snakes and colour them freely. Finally, they trace the numbers with different coloured crayons.

1 Colour the letters. Trace and write.

Present the letter. The children identify and colour the letters "k" in the box. Then the children trace and write the letters with different coloured crayons.

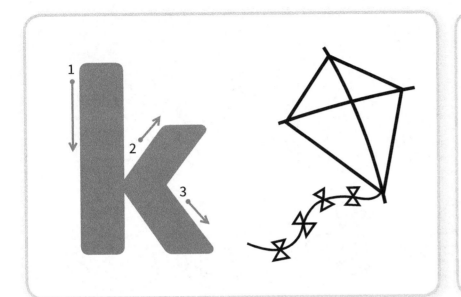

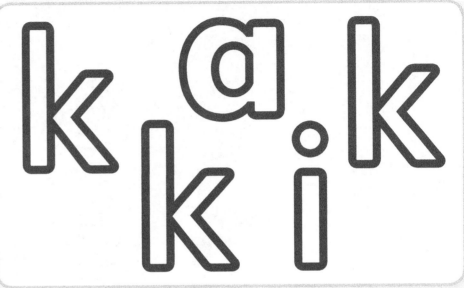

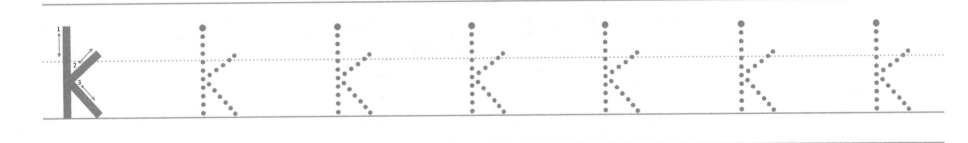

1 **Count and colour the pictures. Trace.**

Present the number. Then the children count the tigers and colour them freely. Finally, they trace the numbers with different coloured crayons.

1 **Find and colour the lion. Trace and write.**

1 # Count and colour the pictures. Trace.

13

14

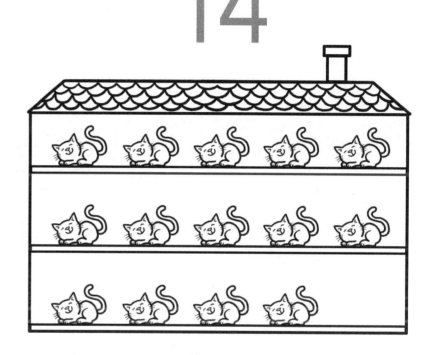

13 13 13 13 13 13 13

14 14 14 14 14 14 14

1 **Listen and circle. Colour the pictures.**

Write the word *log*. The children say /ɒ/ – /ɒ/ – /ɒ/ – *log*. Repeat the procedure with *dot* and *pot*. Next, the children circle the correct word for each picture. Finally, they colour the pictures freely.

l**o**g

p**o**t / d**o**t

d**o**t / p**o**t

1 **Match, glue and colour.**

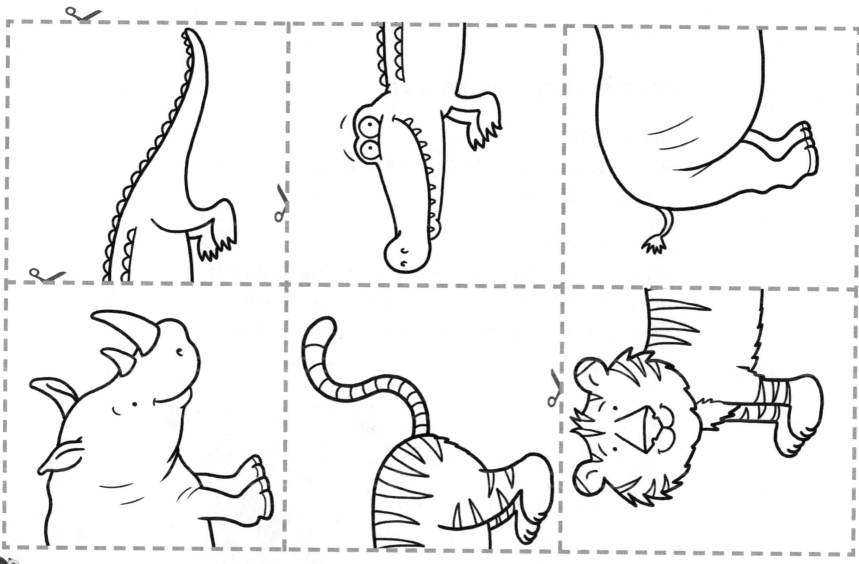

Match, glue and colour.

Materials:
scissors, glue, separate sheet of construction paper, crayons

Instructions:
The children cut out and match the animals' bodies. Then the children glue the animals on a separate sheet of construction paper and colour them.

1 **Look and match.**

 Show the children how to match the close-up of the crocodile with the full picture of the animal. Repeat the procedure for the rest of the shapes and animals.

5 Fruit and vegetables

1 Colour the picture. Trace and write.

Present the letter. Then the children colour the mouse freely. Finally, they trace and write the letters with different coloured crayons.

m

1 **Follow and draw.**

Review the numbers. Then the children follow the lines from the picture to the number, and finally to the box. The children draw the corresponding number of food items in the box.

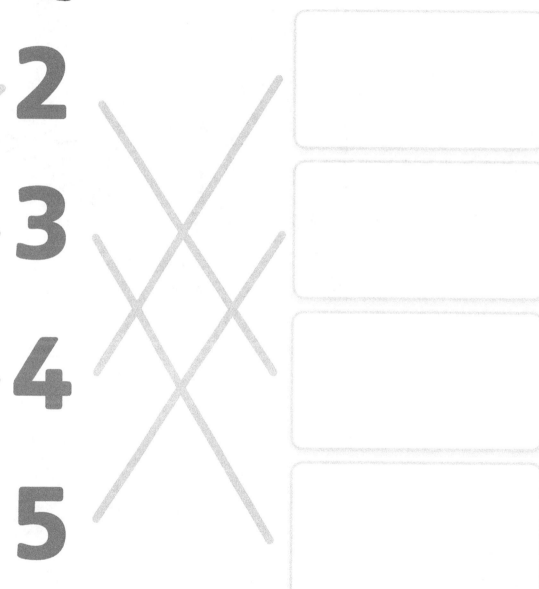

1 **Finger-paint. Trace and write.**

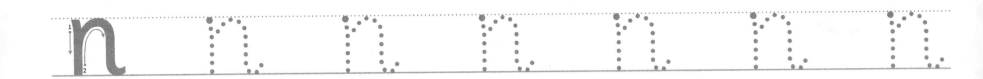

1 Count and circle.

Review the numbers from 1 to 10. The children look at the pictures of the tomatoes. They count the tomatoes aloud and circle the corresponding number. Repeat the procedure for the remaining food items.

6 / 7

8 / 7

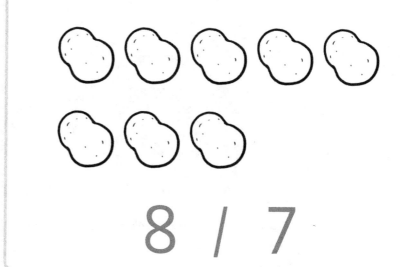

9 / 7

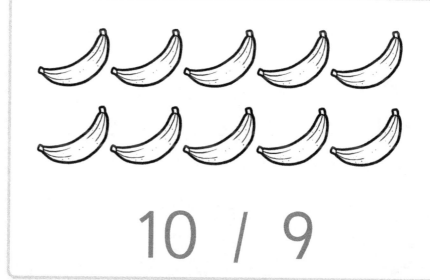

10 / 9

1 ## Colour the letter and the picture. Trace and write.

1 Trace the numbers. Draw.

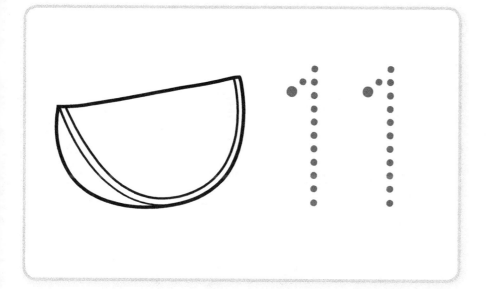

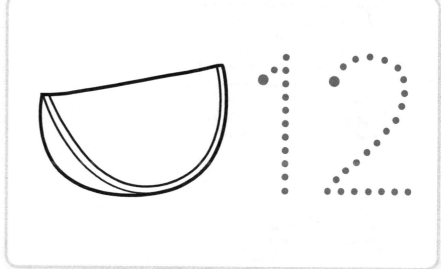

1 **Follow the maze and trace.**

c<u>u</u>p

c<u>u</u>t

b<u>u</u>s

1 **Colour, cut and assemble.**

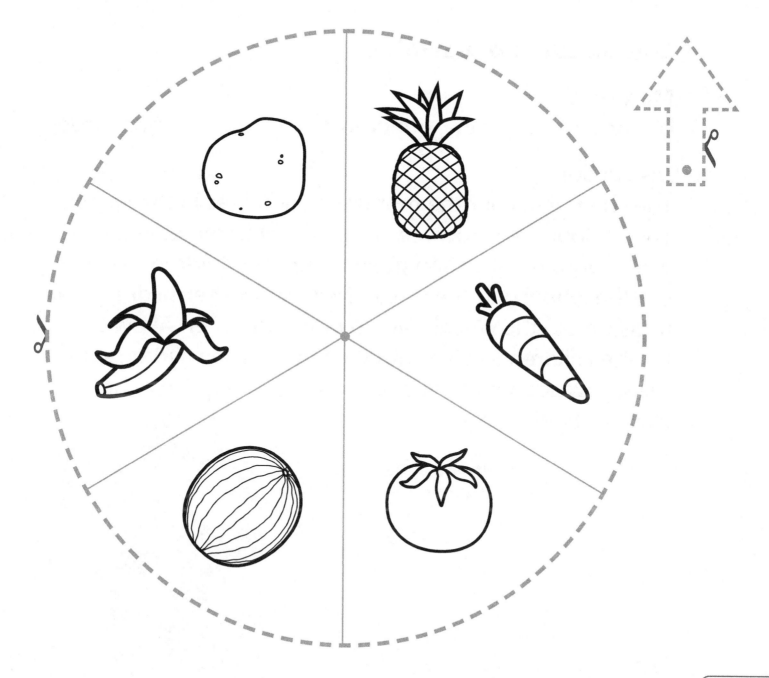

Colour, cut and assemble.

Materials:
crayons, scissors, glue, paper fasteners, construction paper

Instructions:
The children colour the fruit and vegetables in the wheel. They colour the arrow red. Then, the children glue the wheel onto construction paper. Help the children to cut out the wheel and the arrow. Next, show the children how to assemble the wheel using a paper fastener. Allow time for the children to play with the wheel. The children spin the arrow, identify the items, and say if they are either fruit or vegetables.

1 **Listen and colour the pictures.**

 The children colour the fruit and vegetables with different coloured crayons according to your instructions: pineapple – yellow, watermelon – green, tomato – red and carrot – orange.

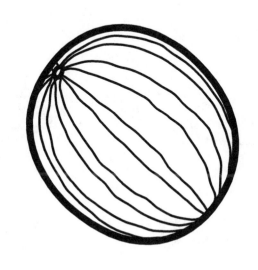

Present the letter. The children colour the pictures of the words that start with the letter "p". Finally, the children trace and write the letters with different coloured crayons.

1 Colour the pictures. Trace and write.

pen   **mouse**   **puppy**

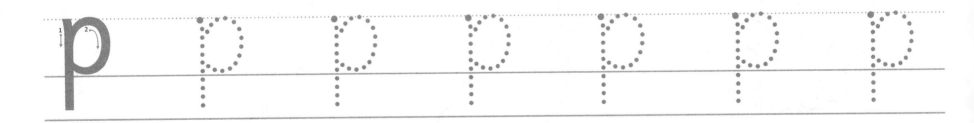

1 Count and colour the pictures. Trace.

Present the number. The children count the slides and colour them freely. Finally, they trace the numbers with different coloured crayons.

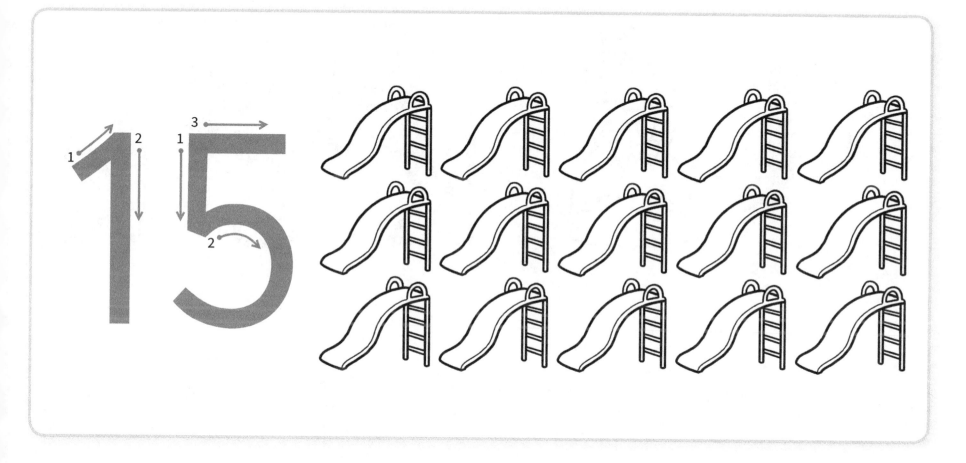

1 **Colour the letters. Trace and write.**

Present the letter. The children identify the letters "q" and colour them. Then the children colour in the picture. Finally, they trace and write the letters with different coloured crayons.

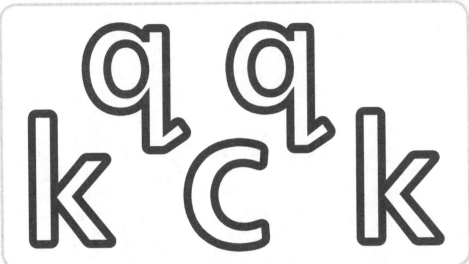

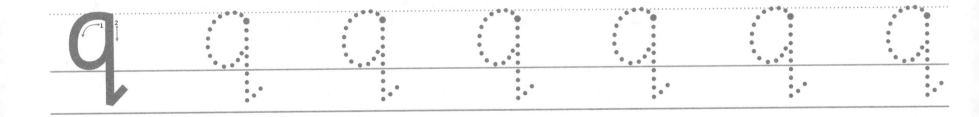

1 **Count and colour the pictures. Trace.**

Present the number. Then children count the robots and colour them freely. Finally, the children trace the numbers with different coloured crayons.

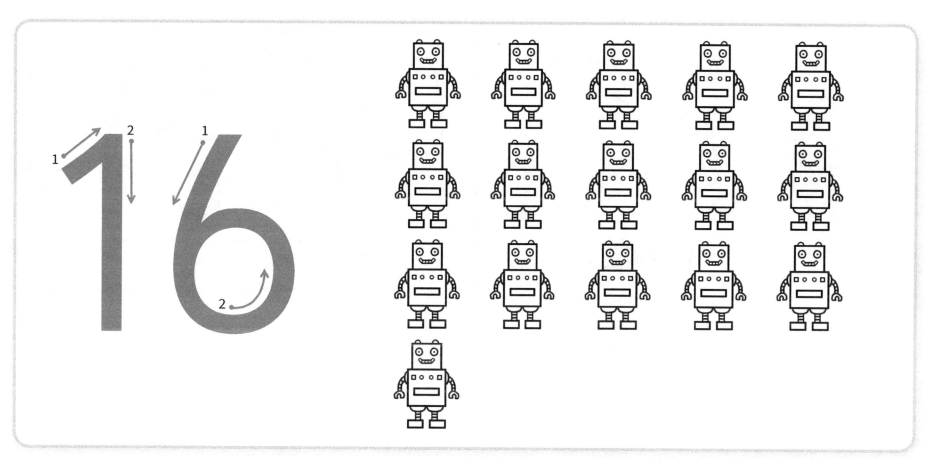

1 **Find and colour the rabbit. Trace and write.**

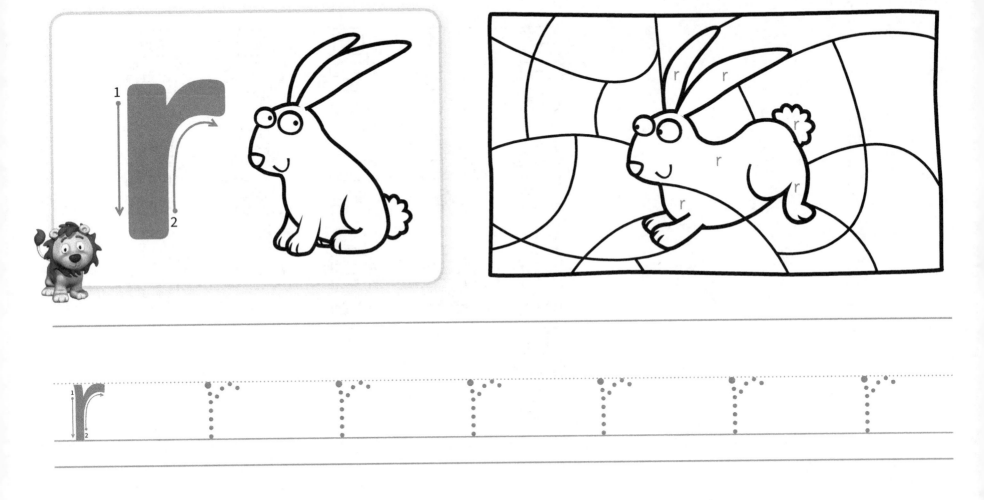

1 Count and draw one more. Trace.

15

16

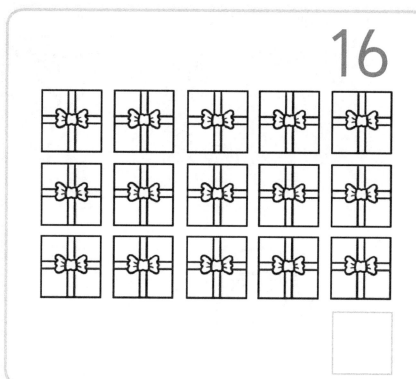

15 15 15 15 15 15 15

16 16 16 16 16 16 16

1 **Look and match.**

The children point to the map. Say /m/ – /m/ – /m/ – *map*. Continue in the same manner with *mum*, *mop* and *marker*. The children identify the pictures on the left and draw lines to match them with the corresponding pictures on the right.

<u>m</u>um

<u>m</u>op

<u>m</u>arker

1 Make a model.

Make a model.

Materials:
waterpaints, paintbrush, construction paper, scissors, tape, glue

Preparation:
Cut small right-angled triangles (5 cm tall) out of construction paper.

Instructions:
The children name the places. The children paint the pictures. Then the children glue the paper onto a piece of construction paper. Help the children cut out the strips.
Then help the children attach the triangles to the back of the strips with tape, so the buildings can stand up to form streets.

1 **Look and trace the path. Colour the picture.**

Ask the children where the boy and girl in the picture are. The children follow the path to the swing. Then the children go to the slide, then to the seesaw, and lastly to the roundabout. Finally, the children trace the path and colour the playground equipment freely.

7 Jobs

Present the letter. The children trace and write the letters with different coloured crayons. Finally, the children colour the sun freely.

1 Trace and write. Colour the picture.

S   S   S   S   S   S   S

S

1 **Count and colour the pictures. Trace.**

Present the number. The children count the helmets and colour them freely. Then the children trace the numbers with different coloured crayons.

1 Finger-paint. Trace and write.

Present the letter. The children dip their fingers in finger paint and print them along the letter "t" and the table. Finally, the children trace and write the letters with different coloured crayons.

1 **Count and colour the pictures. Trace.**

Present the number. Then the children count the pencils and colour them freely. Finally, they trace the numbers with different coloured crayons.

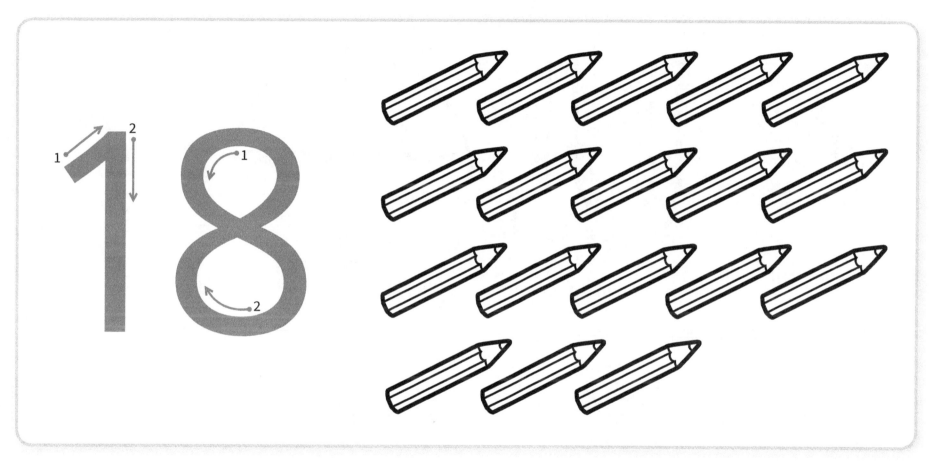

1 **Colour the letter and the picture. Trace and write.**

1 **Trace. Count and colour the pictures.**

Review the numbers. The children trace the numbers with different coloured crayons. Next, the children count the helmets in each set. Finally, the children colour all the helmets freely.

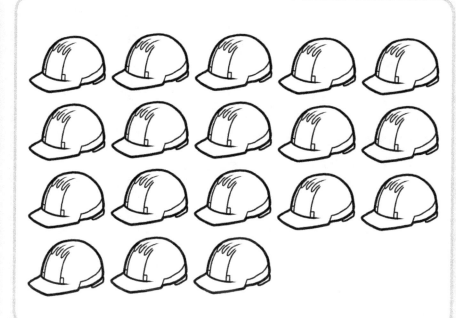

17 17 17 17 17 17 17 17

18 18 18 18 18 18 18

1 **Listen and colour the pictures.**

The children point to the jar. Say /dʒ/ – /dʒ/ – /dʒ/ – jar.
Say *Colour the picture that is the same.* Say *Listen: /dʒ/ – jet; /m/ – map?*
Are they the same? No. Continue in the same manner with the rest of
the activity. The children colour the picture that is the same. Repeat the
procedure for the rest of the activity.

 jet

 jeans

1 Make stick puppets. Role-play.

Make stick puppets. Role-play.

Materials:
construction paper, scissors, glue, coloured crayons, craft sticks

Instructions:
The children look at the community workers and colour them freely. Then the children glue the workers onto a piece of construction paper. Once dry, the children cut out the workers. Next, the children glue a craft stick to the back of each cut-out. Let dry. Finally, the children use their puppets to role-play: *I am a firefighter.*

1 Look and match.

Say *firefighter*. The children repeat. Continue in the same manner with *teacher*, *farmer* and *doctor*. Then the children match the workplaces with the corresponding workers. Then say *This is a hose. Who uses a hose? The firefighter.* Continue in the same manner with the rest of the activity. Finally, the children match the workers with the items they use.

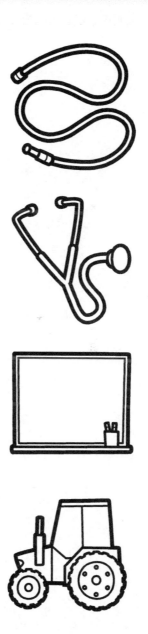

8 The weather

Present the letter. The children colour the picture of the word that starts with letter "v". Finally, the children trace and write the letters with different coloured crayons.

1 Colour the picture. Trace and write.

<u>v</u>an <u>m</u>ouse

1 **Count and colour the pictures. Trace.**

1 **Colour the letters. Trace and write.**

Present the letter. The children identify and colour the letters "w" in the box. Finally, they trace and write the letters with different coloured crayons.

1 ## Count and colour the pictures. Trace.

Present the number. The children count the flowers and colour them freely. Finally, the children trace the numbers with different coloured crayons.

1 **Trace and write. Colour the picture.**

Present the letter. The children trace and write the letters with different coloured crayons. Finally, the children colour the picture freely.

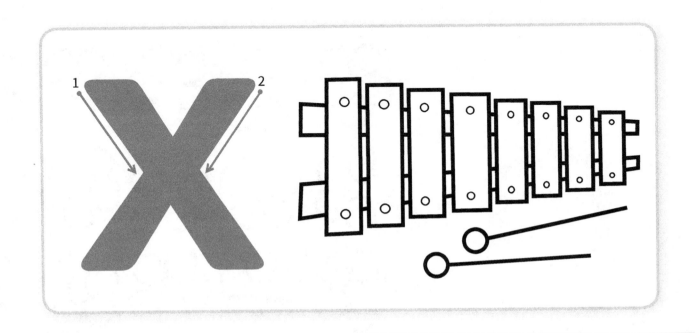

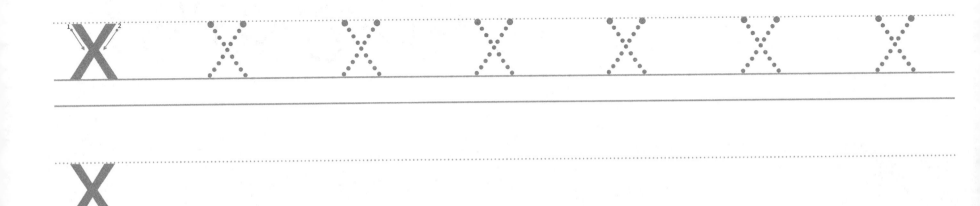

1 **Look and draw. Trace the numbers.**

Review the numbers. Then the children identify the number 19 and draw the corresponding number of snowflakes. Repeat the procedure for the number 20 and the flowers. Finally, the children trace the numbers with different coloured crayons.

19

20

19 19 19 19 19 19 19

20 20 20 20 20 20 20

1 **Listen and trace. Colour the pictures.**

The children point to the log. Say /l/ – /l/ – /l/ – *log*. Continue in the same manner with *lamp* and *lion*. The children identify the pictures in the left column and trace the dotted lines to match the pictures to the words. Finally, the children colour the pictures freely.

log

lamp

lion

1 Make a mobile.

Make a mobile.

Materials:
coloured crayons, construction paper, scissors, cotton balls, glue, plastic clothes hangers, knotted threads of different lengths, hole punch

Preparation:
Make small cotton balls and distribute them among children. Cut knotted threads of different lengths (3 per child).

Instructions:
The children cut out the sun and the clouds and glue them onto a piece of construction paper. Then they colour the sun and glue the cotton balls onto the clouds. Once dry, the children cut out the sun and the clouds. Make a hole at the top of each item with a hole punch. Help the children pull a thread through each hole and tie the sun and the clouds to their clothes hanger.

1 **Look and colour the pictures.**

 Ask *What's the weather like?* The children identify the two kinds of weather: *sunny* and *snowy*. Then the children colour the objects that correspond to each type of weather.

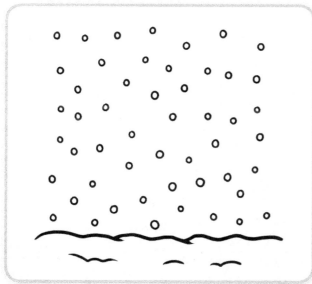

Present the letter. The children trace and write the letters on the lines. Finally, the children colour the picture freely.

1 Trace and write. Colour the picture.

1 **Draw one more and match. Colour the pictures.**

Review the numbers from 1 to 10. Then the children draw one object in each box. Next, the children count the objects aloud and match the objects to the corresponding number. Finally, the children colour the items freely.

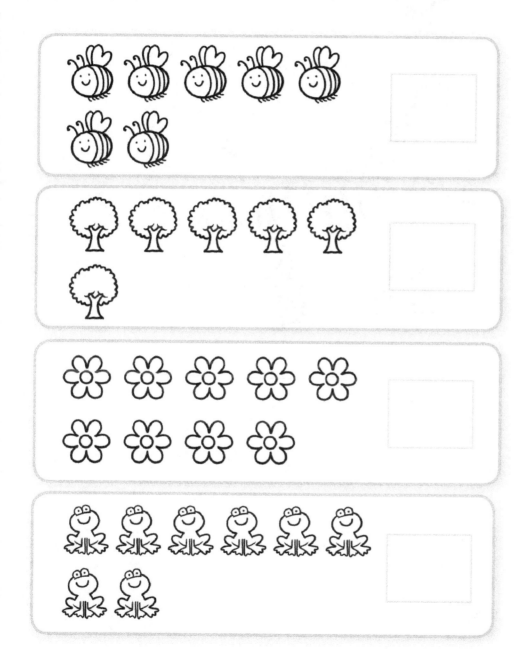

7

8

9

10

1 Finger-paint. Trace and write.

Present the letter. The children dip their fingers in finger paint and print their fingerprints along the letter "z" and the zebra. Then the children trace and write the letters with different coloured crayons.

1 **Count and trace. Colour the pictures.**

Review the numbers from 1 to 15. Then the children count the objects in each box and trace the corresponding number. Finally, the children colour the pictures freely.

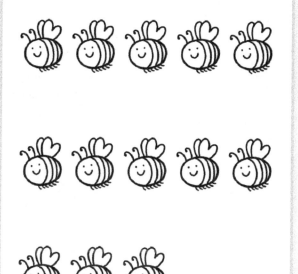

1 Trace the letters. Colour the pictures.

a b c d e

f g h i j k

l m n o p

q r s t u

v x y z

1 Count and trace the numbers.

The children count the lily pads aloud. Next, they trace the numbers.

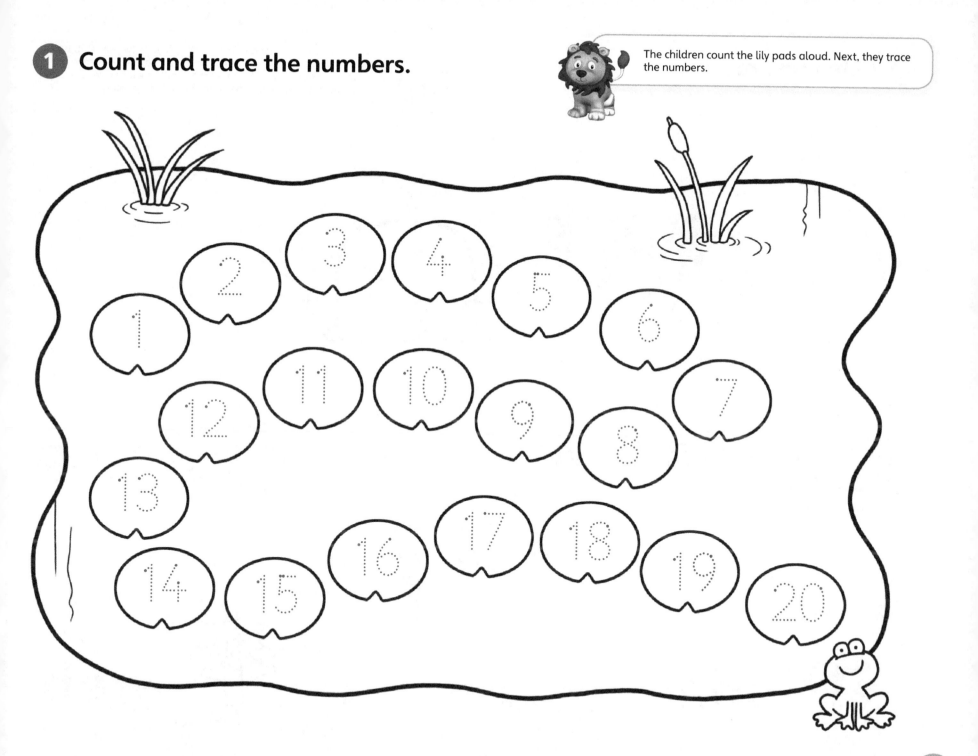

1 **Listen and match.**

Say *Point to the wet whale*. The children follow the instructions. Say /w/ – /w/ – /w/ – *wet*. The children copy. Say /w/ – *window, is it the same sound? Yes!* Match *window* with the letter "w". Continue in the same manner with the rest of the activity.

window

map

pin

web

1 Make a bee.

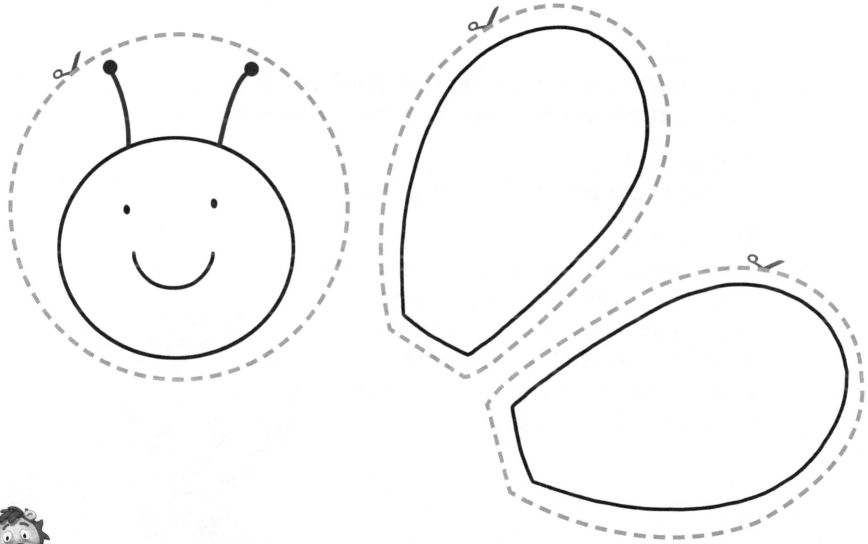

Make a bee.

Materials:
paper plates cut in half (1 half per child), paintbrushes, black and yellow paint, glue, coloured crayons, scissors

Preparation:
Cut paper plates in half (1 half per child).

Instructions:
The children cut out the bee's face and wings and colour them freely. Then they paint the paper plate yellow. Once dry, the children paint black vertical stripes on the bee's body. Finally, they glue the face and the wings onto the bee's body.

1 **Look and match.**

 Say *Point to the big spider.* The children follow the instruction. Continue in the same manner with the rest of the items on the page. Then show the children how to match the big items with the small items using crayons.

Thanks and acknowledgements

The publishers are grateful to the following contributors:

Blooberry Design: cover design, book design, publishing management and
page make-up
Bill Bolton: cover illustration

The publishers and authors are grateful to the following illustrators:

Bill Bolton 1, (1 and repeats on all pages of Leo); Louise Gardner 10, 13, 21,
23, 27, 33, 37, 39, 41, 43, 45, 46, 49, 57, 59, 61, 63, 65, 67, 71, 73, 76, 77, 81, 85,
87, 89, 91, 93, 95; Marek Jagucki 4, 19, 20, 25, 29, 31, 35, 40, 47, 51, 55, 60, 68,
69, 75, 79, 83, 95; Bernice Lum 5, 6, 7, 8, 9, 11, 12, 13, 15, 16, 18, 22, 26, 28, 30,
32, 36, 38, 42, 48, 50, 56, 58, 62, 66, 70, 72, 76, 78, 80, 82, 86, 88, 90, 92